footsteps

kyoto

Be fearless in the pursuit of what sets your soul on fire." – Jennifer Lee.

For KYOTO 京都方面

CPSIA information can be obtained
at www.ICGtesting.com
Printed in the USA
BVHW021346110719
553192BV00014B/358/P

9 780464 022152